The No-Cook Recipe Book

30 of the Most Delicious and Wholesome No-Cook Recipes Ever!

BY: Allie Allen

COOK & ENJOY

Copyright 2019 Allie Allen

Copyright Notes

This book is written as an informational tool. While the author has taken every precaution to ensure the accuracy of the information provided therein, the reader is warned that they assume all risk when following the content. The author will not be held responsible for any damages that may occur as a result of the readers' actions.

The author does not give permission to reproduce this book in any form, including but not limited to: print, social media posts, electronic copies or photocopies, unless permission is expressly given in writing.

Table of Contents

Introduction 6

1. Overnight Oats.. 8

2. Apricot Ricotta Bagels... 10

3. Smoked Salmon Breakfast Crackers 12

4. Peanut Butter Pumpkin Bars 14

5. Avocado Fruit Salad.. 17

6. Pineapple Blueberry Smoothie 20

7. Carrot Soup 22

8. Avocado Coconut Soup 24

9. Marinated Mushroom Salad... 26

10. Curry Deviled Eggs 29

11. Mango Spring Rolls with Almond Dipping Sauce......... 31

12. Shrimp Tacos with Tomatillo Black Bean Salsa 35

13. Shrimp and Noodles with Sweet and Sour Sauce 38

14. Tuna Salad with White Bean Dressing 41

15. Moroccan Chicken Salad 44

16. Chickpea Pitas with Tahini Dressing 47

17. Tex-Mex Chipotle Beans 50

18. Roast Beef Wraps 53

19. Bean Tacos with Cabbage Slaw 56

20. Lentil Wild Rice Pilaf 59

21. Salmon Lentil Stuffed Tomatoes with Curry Sauce 62

22. Lemony Apple Fennel Salad 65

23. Watermelon Salad 68

24. Kale Slaw with Hazelnut Dressing 71

25. Very Berry Parfait Pudding 74

26. BBQ Chicken Sandwiches with Pickled Vegetables 77

27. Blueberry Dessert Soup 81

28. PB&J Pops 84

29. Coffee Ice Cream Float 87

30. Chai Chia Pudding 89

Conclusion... 92

About the Author... 93

Author's Afterthoughts... 95

Introduction

Looking for delicious recipes that won't have you standing and sweating over a simmering pot of food? Or are you looking for recipes that are quick, require no effort but are in no ways, tasteless? If so, it's time to embrace the art of whipping up no-cook meals! With the help of this book, you'll be able to put up easy, gourmet-tasting dishes that require no cooking whatsoever!

Each recipe includes simple ingredients and step-by-step instructions that ensures guaranteed deliciousness. So what are you waiting for? Let's get started!

1. Overnight Oats

In our busy world, few people have time to cook up hearty steel-cut oats in the morning. Thankfully, soaking steel-cut oats overnight softens their texture so they can be enjoyed uncooked. The result is a deliciously chewy and ¬filling breakfast cereal.

Makes: 4 servings

Prep: 5 mins plus overnight

Ingredients:

- 2 cups steel-cut oats
- ½ cup almond flour
- 3 tbsp. chia seeds
- 2 tbsp. pure maple syrup
- 1 tsp. vanilla extract
- 1 tsp. ground cinnamon
- ½ tsp. ground nutmeg
- 2 cups milk of choice, plus more for serving
- 1/2 cup chopped nuts such as walnuts or almonds
- 1 cup berries of choice

Directions:

Add all of the ingredients in a large container and stir until well combined. Cover and refrigerate overnight.

Enjoy!

2. Apricot Ricotta Bagels

These delicious bagels are the perfect lazy-day breakfast option. This recipe is good with other stone fruits like peaches, nectarines, or plums.

Makes: 2 servings

Prep: 5-10 mins

Ingredients:

- 1 cup low-fat ricotta cheese
- 1 tbsp. honey
- 1/2 tsp. ground cinnamon
- 1/2 tsp. vanilla extract
- 2 bagels of choice, sliced in half
- 4 fresh apricots, thinly sliced
- 1/4 cup coarsely chopped pistachios

Directions:

In a small bowl, stir the ricotta cheese, honey, cinnamon and vanilla together. Toast the bagel halves.

Spread the cheese mixture on the toasted bagels, and top with apricot slices and pistachios.

Enjoy!

3. Smoked Salmon Breakfast Crackers

Smoked salmon is a much-enjoyed brunch item for many. Try it with this sweet and creamy avocado spread and you'll be a convert, too.

Makes: 2-4 servings

Prep: 5 mins

Ingredients:

- 1 medium ripe avocado
- 4 ounces cream cheese
- 1 tbsp. honey
- 1 tsp. grated orange zest
- Pinch of sea salt
- 8 rye crackers or crispbreads
- 4 to 6 ounces smoked salmon
- 1 tbsp. chopped chives

Directions:

In a medium bowl, mash the avocado using a fork. Add in the cream cheese, honey, orange zest and salt and stir with a spoon until well combined.

Spread the avocado mixture on the crackers, and top with smoked salmon and chives.

Enjoy!

4. Peanut Butter Pumpkin Bars

A medley of carefully matched ingredients ensures that each bite of these moist no-bake bars is tastier than the last.

Makes: 6-12 servings

Prep: 10 mins plus 1 hr.

Ingredients:

- 2 tbsp. molasses
- 2 cups granola of choice, plus more for topping
- 3/4 cup of unsalted and natural peanut butter or you can use other nut butter of choice
- ½ cup oat bran
- ½ cup non-instant milk powder
- ½ tsp. ground cinnamon
- 1/3 cup dried currants
- 3/4 cup canned pumpkin puree
- ½ tsp. ground ginger
- ¼ tsp. ground cloves
- Pinch of sea salt

Directions:

Line an 8 x 8 inch baking pan with a parchment paper.

Place the peanut butter, pumpkin and molasses in a large bowl and mix until well combined. Add in the remaining ingredients and mix until everything is moist. The mixture should be thick.

Place the mixture the prepared pan and spread it out until you have an even thickness of about 1/2 inch. Sprinkle some additional granola on top and press down lightly. Place the pan in the freezer for about 1 hour.

Slice into bars and store in an airtight container in the refrigerator.

Enjoy!

5. Avocado Fruit Salad

Here's a fresh and delicious recipe to add some flair to brunch time. Nutritious avocado adds a creamy textural contrast to this fruit salad and helps cut some of the acidity.

Makes: 4 servings

Prep: 10 mins

Ingredients:

- 1 large orange
- 1 large banana, thinly sliced
- 2 kiwifruits, peeled and sliced
- 1 cup blackberries
- 1 ripe large avocado, cubed
- 1/4 cup chopped walnuts
- 1/4 cup coconut flakes
- Zest of 1 lime
- Juice of 1 lime, divided
- 1 1/2 cups plain, low-fat yogurt
- 2 tbsp. honey
- 1 tsp. vanilla extract or orange extract
- 1/4 cup cacao nibs (optional)

Directions:

Peel the orange, separate into segments, and slice each segment into thirds. Add to a large bowl and toss with the banana, kiwifruit, blackberries, avocado, walnuts, coconut flakes, lime zest and half of the lime juice.

In a small bowl, whisk together the yogurt, remaining lime juice, honey and vanilla or orange extract. Spoon the fruit mixture into serving bowls, and top with the yogurt mixture and cocoa nibs if using.

Enjoy!

6. Pineapple Blueberry Smoothie

Along with whole grain quinoa flakes, tangy coconut water, healthy fat from almonds and the protein in the egg whites, this drink is a complete nutritional and delicious package.

Makes: 2 servings

Prep: 5 mins

Ingredients:

- 2 cups coconut water
- 1 cup pineapple chunks
- 1/3 cup quinoa flakes
- 1/2 cup pasteurized egg whites
- 1/4 cup unsalted raw or roasted almonds
- 1 tsp. vanilla extract or 1/2 tsp. almond extract
- 1/4 tsp. ground cloves
- 1 cup frozen blueberries

Direction:

Place all ingredients in a blender's container and then blend until smooth, about 30 seconds.

Divide between two glasses and serve.

Enjoy!

7. Carrot Soup

A sweet, spicy and earthy soup recipe with maple syrup, ginger and pecans.

Makes: 4 servings

Prep: 2 hrs. + 5 mins

Ingredients:

- 2 cups apple juice
- 1/2 cup water
- 1 pound carrots (about 6 to 7 medium), peeled and chopped
- 1 cup plain yogurt
- 2 tbsp. pure maple syrup
- 2 tsp. chopped fresh ginger
- 1 tsp. ground allspice
- 1/4 tsp. sea salt
- 1/8 tsp. cayenne
- 1/4 cup sliced pecans, for garnish

Directions:

Place all the ingredients except the pecans in a blender or food processor container and blend until very smooth, about 1 minute. Refrigerate for at least 2 hours before serving.

To serve, ladle the soup into serving bowls and garnish with pecans.

Enjoy!

8. Avocado Coconut Soup

Avocado lends this soup a creamy texture, while coconut milk gives it a fresh and tropical flavor.

Makes: 4 servings

Prep: 2 hrs. + 5 mins

Ingredients:

- 1 1/2 cups coconut milk
- 1 1/2 cups water
- 2 ripe large avocados
- 1/4 cup packed fresh basil
- Juice of 1 lime
- 1 jalapeño chili pepper, seeded and minced
- 1/4 tsp. sea salt
- 1/4 tsp. freshly ground pepper, preferably white
- Grated zest of 1 lime

Directions:

Place all the ingredients except the lime zest in a blender or food processor container and blend until smooth. If the mixture is too thick, simply blend in more coconut milk or water.

Pour the mixture into a container with a tight-¬fitting lid and refrigerate for at least 2 hours.

When ready to serve, ladle the soup into serving bowls and garnish with lime zest.

Enjoy!

9. Marinated Mushroom Salad

A delicious marinated mushroom salad with cherry tomatoes, thyme and walnuts.

Makes: 4 servings

Prep: 10 mins plus chilling time

Ingredients: 2 hrs. + 10 mins

- 1 ½ cups cherry tomatoes, sliced in half
- 4 tbsp. extra virgin olive oil
- 4 cups of cremini mushrooms, sliced thinly
- 3 tbsp. white wine or 2 tbsp. white wine vinegar
- 1 clove garlic, minced
- 2 tsp. Dijon mustard
- 2 tsp. fresh thyme
- 1 tsp. fennel seeds (optional)
- 1/2 tsp. sea salt
- 1/4 tsp. freshly ground black pepper
- 1/3 cup coarsely chopped ¬at-leaf parsley
- 2 cups of spinach or other greens of choice
- 1/3 cup chopped walnuts, for garnish
- 4 tbsp. grated Parmesan or Gruyere cheese, for garnish
- Truffle oil, for garnish (optional)

Directions:

In a large bowl or container, combine the mushrooms and tomatoes. In a separate bowl, whisk together the oil, wine or vinegar, garlic, mustard, thyme, fennel seeds if using, salt and black pepper.

Add the oil mixture to the mushrooms and tomatoes and toss to coat. Cover and let marinate in the refrigerator for at least 2 hours or up to overnight, stirring a couple of times.

Mix the parsley into the mushroom mixture. Arrange the spinach on serving plates and top with mushroom salad. Garnish with walnuts, grated cheese, and truffle oil if desired.

Enjoy!

10. Curry Deviled Eggs

This curry is absolutely delicious and a guaranteed crowd favorite.

Makes: 6 servings

Prep: 10 mins

Ingredients:

- 6 jarred pickled eggs
- 1/3 cup sour cream
- 1 green onion (scallion), green part only, thinly sliced or 1 tbsp. chopped chives
- 1 tsp. creamy Dijon mustard or regular yellow mustard
- 1 tsp. curry powder
- 1/2 tsp. paprika, preferably smoked, plus more for garnish
- 1/4 tsp. freshly ground black pepper

Directions:

Slice each egg in half and scoop the yolks out and place them into a medium bowl. Using the back of a fork, mash the yolks. Stir in the remaining ingredients until smooth.

Spoon the yolk mixture in to the egg cavities or use a piping bag.

Sprinkle with paprika and refrigerate until ready to serve.

Enjoy!

11. Mango Spring Rolls with Almond Dipping Sauce

Handy Vietnamese rice paper wrappers are ideal for making refreshing and chic-looking appetizer or light lunch rolls. The nutty almond dipping sauce ups the ante on an already great dish.

Makes: 8 servings

Prep: 10-15 mins

Ingredients:

For the spring rolls:

- 2 ounces dried rice vermicelli noodles
- 16 round rice paper wrappers
- 1 large mango, peeled and cut into strips
- 1 small red bell pepper, thinly sliced
- 1 medium avocado, thinly sliced
- 16 fresh mint leaves, sliced in half

For the dipping sauce:

- 1/4 cup unsalted almond butter
- 2 tsp. grated or finely minced fresh ginger
- 1/4 cup coconut milk
- 2 cloves garlic, grated or finely minced
- 2 tbsp. reduced-sodium soy sauce
- 2 tbsp. rice vinegar
- 1 tsp. honey
- 2 tsp. chili sauce, such as Sriracha

Directions:

For the spring rolls: Bring 4 cups water to a boil using an electric kettle. Place the rice vermicelli noodles in a large heatproof bowl and pour the boiled water over the top. Allow the noodles to soak for 3 minutes. Drain and rinse under cold water. Place the noodles on a cutting board and slice into thirds so the noodles are about 2 inches long.

Fill a skillet or shallow pan with hot water; the pan should be large enough so the rice papers can lie flat. Fully submerge one rice paper wrapper in the water and soak until softened, about 20 seconds.

Lay the softened wrapper flat on a cutting board or other clean work surface. Place a small bunch of vermicelli noodles in the bottom one-third of the wrapper, leaving about 1-inch free along the bottom edge. Lay three strips of mango, two strips of red pepper, and one slice of avocado over the noodles.

Top with about 4 mint halves. Begin tightly rolling the wrapper and filling away from you. Fold in the left and right sides of the wrapper. Finish rolling tightly, and slice in half on the bias. Repeat with the remaining rice wrappers and filling.

For the dipping sauce: Whisk all the sauce ingredients together in a medium bowl until smooth. Serve the mango rolls with sauce on the side.

Enjoy!

12. Shrimp Tacos with Tomatillo Black Bean Salsa

The tart, apple-flavored flesh of the tomatillo punches up the light and refreshing salsa in this recipe.

Makes: 4 servings

Prep: 10 mins

Ingredients:

For Salsa:

- 2 cups diced tomatillo
- 1 cup cubed pineapple
- 1 cup canned black beans, rinsed and drained
- 1/2 small red onion, diced finely
- 1 jalapeño chili pepper, seeded, minced
- 2 cloves garlic, minced
- 1/2 cup chopped cilantro
- Juice of 1 lime
- 1/2 tsp. ground cumin
- 1/4 tsp. sea salt

For the tacos:

- 1/2 pound frozen and thawed cooked shrimp
- 8 (6 to 8-inch) corn or whole wheat tortillas

Directions:

For the salsa: In a large bowl, toss together the tomatillo, pineapple, black beans, onion, chili pepper, garlic, cilantro, lime juice, cumin and salt.

For the tacos: Divide the shrimp among the tortillas and top with the salsa.

Enjoy!

13. Shrimp and Noodles with Sweet and Sour Sauce

Reminiscent of pad Thai, this no-fuss noodle dish is the perfect option for harried weeknights or for when you need a quick and nutritious lunch.

Makes: 4-6 servings

Prep: 40 mins

Ingredients:

- 1/2 box (about 8 ounces) wide Thai rice noodles
- 2 tbsp. chopped tamarind pulp or rice vinegar
- 2 tbsp. reduced-sodium soy sauce or tamari
- 1 1/2 tbsp. fish sauce
- 1 tbsp. sesame oil
- 1 tbsp. coconut palm sugar, brown sugar, or honey
- 1 clove garlic, finely minced
- 1-inch piece fresh ginger or galangal, finely minced
- 2 dried Thai bird chili peppers, crushed or 1/4 tsp. dried red chili flakes
- 2 medium carrots, peeled and sliced into thin matchsticks
- 2 green onions (scallions), white and green parts, thinly sliced
- 2 cups bean sprouts
- 1 pound medium or large cooked frozen shrimp, thawed and shelled
- 1/3 cup coarsely chopped unsalted roasted peanuts
- 1/4 cup coarsely chopped cilantro or Thai basil
- 1 lime, sliced into wedges

Directions:

Place the noodles in a large heatproof bowl. Bring a full kettle of water to a boil and then pour over the noodles until fully covered. Let stand, stirring occasionally, until the noodles soften and become tender, 20 to 25 minutes. Drain well and place the noodles back in the bowl.

Meanwhile, if using tamarind place the pulp in a small bowl and mix with 4 tbsp. very hot water. Let soak for 10 minutes. Mash the tamarind with the back of a fork in the soaking water, press the mixture through a ¬net-mesh sieve, and reserve the tamarind water.

Stir together the tamarind water or rice vinegar with the soy sauce, ¬fish sauce, sesame oil, sweetener, garlic, ginger, and chili pepper.

Add the dressing to the noodles and toss to coat. Taste and adjust seasonings as desired.

Add the carrot, green onion, and bean sprouts to the noodles and toss to combine. Divide the noodle mixture among serving plates, and top with the shrimp, peanuts, and cilantro or basil. Serve with lime wedges. Enjoy!

14. Tuna Salad with White Bean Dressing

Influenced by Mediterranean flavors, this salad is a beautiful display of rainbow colors on your plate. And it tastes just as good as it looks!

Makes: 4 servings

Prep: 10 mins

Ingredients:

For the salad:

- 6 cups leafy vegetables, such as lettuce, spinach and radicchio
- 1 large red or orange bell pepper, thinly sliced
- 1 cup halved cherry tomatoes
- 1 large avocado, thinly sliced
- 2 (5-ounce) cans albacore tuna, drained
- 1/3 cup pitted and sliced Kalamata olives
- 2 tbsp. capers

For the dressing:

- 1 cup canned white navy beans, rinsed and drained
- 1/2 cup plain yogurt
- 1 cup packed flatleaf parsley
- 2 tbsp. tahini
- 1 tsp. Dijon mustard
- Juice of 1/2 lemon
- 2 cloves garlic, finely chopped
- 1/4 tsp. sea salt
- 1/4 tsp. freshly ground black pepper

Directions:

For the salad: In a big bowl, toss the greens, bell pepper, cherry tomatoes and avocado together.

Break the tuna meat into chunks with a fork. Divide the salad among serving plates, and top with the tuna chunks, olives and capers.

For the dressing: Place all the dressing ingredients into a blender or food processor container and blend until smooth. Taste and adjust seasonings as needed. Drizzle over the salad.

Enjoy!

15. Moroccan Chicken Salad

Make this highly textured salad on a lazy weekend afternoon and you'll be set for several exciting workday lunches or quick dinners.

Makes: 4-6 servings

Prep: 10-15 mins

Ingredients:

For the salad:

- 1 cup water
- 1 cup couscous, preferably whole wheat
- 1/2 tsp. saffron threads
- 1/4 tsp. sea salt
- 2 to 3 cups diced cooked rotisserie chicken
- 1 medium carrot, peeled and thinly sliced
- 1 cup halved cherry tomatoes
- 1/2 English cucumber, chopped
- 2 green onions (scallions), white and green parts, thinly sliced
- 1/4 cup coarsely chopped fresh mint or cilantro
- 1/2 cup coarsely chopped dried apricots
- 1/3 cup unsalted slivered almonds

For the dressing:

- 1/4 cup extra virgin olive oil or almond oil
- 2 tbsp. ras el hanout spice mixture
- 1 tsp. grated lemon zest
- Juice of 1/2 lemon

Directions:

For the salad: Bring water to a boil using an electric kettle. In a large heatproof bowl, stir 1 cup boiled water with the couscous, saffron and salt. Cover and let stand until the water has been absorbed, about 5 minutes. Fluff couscous with a fork and let cool to room temperature.

Add the chicken, carrot, cherry tomatoes, cucumber, green onion, mint or cilantro, apricots, and almonds to the bowl with the couscous and stir to combine.

For the dressing: In a small bowl, whisk together the oil, ras el hanout, lemon zest, and lemon juice.

Add the dressing to the couscous salad and stir to combine.

Enjoy!

16. Chickpea Pitas with Tahini Dressing

These chickpea pitas are an amazing lunch option, especially with the insanely delicious and creamy tahini dressing.

Makes: 4 servings

Prep: 10 mins

Ingredients:

- 1 (14-ounce) can chickpeas, rinsed and drained
- 1 small red bell pepper, diced
- 1/2 English cucumber, diced
- 2 Roma (plum) tomatoes, seeds removed and chopped
- 1 small red onion, finely diced
- 1/2 cup cilantro or parsley, chopped
- 4 ounces cubed feta cheese
- 1/3 cup black olives, chopped
- 4 tbsp. raisins
- 2 tbsp. tahini
- 3 tbsp. extra virgin olive oil
- Juice of 1 lemon
- 1/2 tsp. ground cumin
- 2 cloves garlic
- 1/4 tsp. cayenne
- 1/4 tsp. sea salt
- 1 tbsp. water
- 1/4 tsp. black pepper
- 4 (6-inch) whole grain pitas, sliced in half

Directions:

In a big bowl, toss together the bell pepper, chickpeas, tomato, cucumber, cilantro or parsley, red onion, feta cheese, raisins and olives.

Place the olive oil, lemon juice, tahini, cumin, garlic, black pepper, salt, cayenne and water in a blender, and blend until they are smooth. Add in the tahini mixture to the chickpea mixture and then stir to coat.

To serve, stuff the chickpea mixture into pitas.

Enjoy!

17. Tex-Mex Chipotle Beans

Replace your boring bean salad recipe with this cheesy and creamy Tex-Mex chipotle beans recipe. The fiber-packed dish also makes for wonderful leftovers.

Makes: 6 servings

Prep: 10 mins

Ingredients:

- 1 (14-ounce) can each white navy beans, kidney beans and black beans, rinsed and drained
- 1 large red bell pepper, chopped
- 1 large avocado, diced
- 1 cup corn kernels, canned or frozen and thawed
- 1/4 cup hemp seeds (optional)
- 1 pound tomatoes (about 3 medium), quartered
- 1/2 small red onion, finely diced (about 1/3 cup)
- 1/3 cup packed cilantro
- 1 tbsp. chopped chipotle chili pepper in the adobo sauce
- 1 clove garlic, chopped
- Juice of 1/2 lime
- 1 tsp. ground cumin
- 1/4 tsp. sea salt
- 1/4 tsp. freshly ground black pepper
- 1/2 cup sour cream
- 1 cup grated sharp cheddar cheese or pepper Jack cheese
- 1 cup coarsely crushed tortilla chips

Directions:

In a large bowl, toss together the beans, bell pepper, avocado, corn and hemp seeds, if using.

Add the tomato, onion, cilantro, chipotle chili pepper, garlic, lime juice, cumin, black pepper and salt to a blender or food processor container and pulse until well combined but still slightly chunky.

Pulse in the sour cream. Pour the tomato mixture over the beans and stir to coat. Stir in the cheese and tortilla chips. Serve at room temperature or chilled.

Enjoy!

18. Roast Beef Wraps

This recipe combines roast beef with a rich and tangy Asian sauce to give you a delicious lunch recipe is less than 10 minutes.

Makes: 4 servings

Prep: 10 mins

Ingredients:

For the sauce:

- 1/3 cup hoisin sauce
- 2 tbsp. honey
- 1 ½ tbsp. soy sauce
- 1 ½ tsp. Chinese five spice powder
- 1 clove garlic, grated or very finely minced
- Grated zest of 1 lemon
- ¼ tsp. freshly ground black pepper
- 1/8 tsp. cayenne, or to taste

For the wraps:

- 4 large tortilla wraps
- 2 cups greens such as baby spinach, watercress, or arugula
- ½ pound thinly sliced roast beef
- 1 cup sliced jarred roasted red pepper
- 1 cup sprouts such as broccoli, alfalfa, or onion (optional)

Directions:

For the sauce: In a medium bowl, whisk together the hoisin sauce, honey, soy sauce, Chinese ¬five spice powder, garlic, lemon zest, black pepper and cayenne.

For the wraps: Lay the tortillas flat on a work surface and spread the hoisin mixture over the entire surface of each. Top with an equal amount of greens, roast beef, roasted red pepper, and sprouts if using. Tightly roll up the tortillas, insert a toothpick at each end, and slice the wraps in half on the bias.

Serve immediately or refrigerate for later use.

Enjoy!

19. Bean Tacos with Cabbage Slaw

Crunchy and creamy at the same time, this dish is perfect for your next taco night.

Makes: 4 servings

Prep: 15 mins

Ingredients:

- 2 cups of shredded red cabbage
- 1 cup shredded carrot
- 2 tbsp. rice vinegar
- 2 tbsp. sweet chili sauce, such as Thai Kitchen
- 2 tbsp. neutral-tasting oil such as canola or grapeseed
- 2 (15-ounce) cans pinto beans, rinsed, drained
- 1 large avocado, cubed
- 1 tsp. ground cumin
- 2 green onions (scallions) sliced thinly (white and green parts)
- 1/3 cup chopped cilantro
- 2/3 cup sour cream
- 1/4 tsp. chipotle or other chili powder
- Juice of 1/2 lime
- 12 hard shell tacos

Directions:

In a big bowl, toss the cabbage and carrot together. In a small bowl, whisk together the rice vinegar, chili sauce and oil. Add the vinegar mixture to the cabbage mixture and toss to coat. Set aside.

In a separate bowl, toss together the beans, avocado, cumin, green onion and cilantro. In another separate bowl, stir together the sour cream, chili powder and lime juice. Taste and add more chili powder if desired.

Stuff each taco with bean mixture, and top with slaw and sour cream sauce.

Enjoy!

20. Lentil Wild Rice Pilaf

This wild and wonderful take on pilaf requires no cooking, just a little patience as you let the wild rice soak until it has a pleasant chewy texture.

Makes: 6 servings

Prep: Top be prepped 3 days in advance + 10 mins

Ingredients:

- 1 cup wild rice
- 2 (15-ounce) cans lentils, rinsed and drained
- 2 celery stalks, thinly sliced
- 1 large apple, diced
- Seeds of 1 pomegranate
- 1/3 cup chopped walnuts or pecans
- 2 green onions (scallions), white and green parts, thinly sliced
- 2 tbsp. fresh marjoram or oregano
- 3 tbsp. extra virgin olive oil or walnut oil
- 2 tbsp. red wine vinegar
- 1/4 tsp. sea salt
- 2 cloves garlic, finely minced
- 1/4 tsp. freshly ground black pepper
- 1/4 tsp. red chili flakes

Directions:

Place the wild rice in a glass container and cover with water. Let soak about 3 days, or until tender and chewy. Ideally, try and change the water once or twice daily.

In a large bowl, toss together the soaked wild rice, lentils, celery, apple, pomegranate seeds, nuts, green onion and marjoram or oregano. In a small bowl, whisk together the oil, vinegar, garlic, salt, black pepper and chili flakes. Add the dressing to the salad and toss to mix.

Enjoy!

21. Salmon Lentil Stuffed Tomatoes with Curry Sauce

Salmon and green lentils are stuffed into fresh beefsteak tomatoes for a wholesome and delicious meal.

Makes: 4 servings

Prep: 10 mins

Ingredients:

- 1 cup canned green lentils, rinsed and drained
- 1 (6-ounce) can salmon, drained or 1 (6-ounce) salmon pouch
- 1 celery stalk, thinly sliced
- 2 red radishes, diced
- 2 tbsp. capers (optional)
- Juice of 1/2 lemon plus 1 additional tsp. fresh lemon juice, divided
- 1 clove garlic, minced
- 2 tbsp. chopped fresh dill
- 1–2 tsp. Dijon mustard
- 1 tsp. fennel seeds (optional)
- 1/4 tsp. sea salt
- 1/4 tsp. freshly ground black pepper
- 2 tbsp. extra virgin olive oil
- 1/2 cup plain, low-fat yogurt
- 1 tsp. curry powder
- 4 large beefsteak tomatoes

Directions:

In a large bowl, toss together the lentils, salmon, celery, radish and capers if using.

In a small bowl, whisk together the juice of 1/2 lemon, garlic, dill, mustard, fennel seeds if using, salt and pepper. Whisk in the olive oil. Add the olive oil mixture to the salmon and lentil mixture and combine gently. In a small bowl, stir together the yogurt, curry powder and remaining 1 tsp. lemon juice.

Slice 1/4 inch off the tops of the tomatoes and guide a small knife around the interior. Use a spoon to scoop out the innards of each tomato. Fill the tomatoes with the salmon and lentil mixture and top with curry yogurt sauce.

Enjoy!

22. Lemony Apple Fennel Salad

With its slight licorice flavor and crunchy texture, fennel is wonderful served raw in salads and it tastes even better combined with apples, arugula and zucchini.

Makes: 4 servings

Prep: 10 mins

For the salad:

- 1 fennel bulb, thinly sliced, fronds reserved for garnish
- 2 medium apples, thinly sliced
- 2 cups packed arugula
- 1 medium zucchini, shredded (about 1 cup)
- 1/4 cup chopped fresh mint (optional)

For the dressing:

- 3 tbsp. extra virgin olive oil
- 1 tbsp. honey
- Juice of 1/2 lemon
- 1 tsp. grated lemon zest
- 1 clove garlic, minced
- 1/4 tsp. sea salt
- 1/4 tsp. freshly ground black pepper

Directions:

For the salad: In a large bowl, toss together the fennel, apple, arugula, zucchini, and mint if using.

For the dressing: In a small bowl, whisk together the olive oil, honey, lemon juice, lemon zest, garlic, salt, and pepper.

Toss the salad with the dressing and serve garnished with fennel fronds.

Enjoy!

23. Watermelon Salad

Providing a salty-sweet cool crunch, this salad featuring watermelon is tantamount to summer on a plate.

Makes: 4 servings

Prep: 10 mins

Ingredients:

- 5 cups seedless watermelon, sliced into 1-inch cubes
- 2 cups thinly sliced jicama or cucumbers
- 1 medium avocado, cubed
- 1 cup cubed feta cheese (about 3 ounces)
- 1/2 cup unsalted raw or roasted whole cashews
- 1/4 cup chopped fresh basil
- 2 tbsp. chopped fresh mint
- 2 tbsp. extra virgin olive oil
- Juice of 1/2 lemon
- 1/2 tsp. freshly ground black pepper
- 1/2 tsp. salt
- 1/4 tsp. red pepper ¬flakes

Directions:

In a large bowl, gently toss together the watermelon, jicama, avocado, feta cheese, cashews, basil and mint.

In a small bowl, whisk together the olive oil, lemon juice, salt, pepper, and pepper flakes. Toss the watermelon and jicama mixture with the dressing. If time permits, chill for about 1 hour before serving.

Enjoy!

24. Kale Slaw with Hazelnut Dressing

This delicious combination of kale, kohlrabi, hazelnuts and fruit is rich, buttery, sweet and fresh.

Makes: 6 servings

Prep: 15-20 mins

Ingredients:

- 1 medium kohlrabi, peeled and shredded (about 1 cup)
- 1/4 tsp. plus 1/8 tsp. sea salt, divided
- 6 cups kale (about 1/2 bunch)
- 1/3 cup whole hazelnuts
- 2 tbsp. cider vinegar
- 1 tsp. grated orange zest
- 1 tsp. grainy mustard
- 2 tsp. fresh thyme
- 1 clove garlic, minced
- 1/4 tsp. freshly ground black pepper
- 1/3 cup extra virgin olive oil
- 1 large red or orange bell pepper, thinly sliced
- 2 medium carrots, peeled and shredded
- 2 medium apples or pears, thinly sliced
- 1/3 cup dried cranberries or cherries
- Parmesan cheese, shaved (optional)

Directions:

Place the kohlrabi in a small bowl, toss with 1/8 tsp. of the salt and let sit 10 minutes. Squeeze out as much water as possible and set aside.

Fold each leaf of kale in half lengthwise and slice out the center rib. Discard the ribs. Roll a stack of the leaves and slice in half lengthwise, then crosswise into very fine ribbons. Add to a large bowl.

Place the hazelnuts, cider vinegar, orange zest, mustard, thyme, garlic, remaining 1/4 tsp. salt, pepper, and olive oil in a food processor or blender container, and blend until well combined but still slightly chunky.

Toss together the kale and hazelnut dressing. With clean hands, firmly massage the greens for about 1 minute, or until tender. Add the kohlrabi, bell pepper, carrot, apple or pear, and dried cranberries or cherries to the kale, and toss to mix. Place on serving plates and garnish with shaved Parmesan if desired.

Enjoy!

25. Very Berry Parfait Pudding

Here's a simple yet classy guilt-free snack that includes grated dark chocolate, fresh mint, and whole berries.

Makes: 4 servings

Prep: 10 mins

Ingredients:

- 2 cups fresh or frozen and thawed mixed berries such as blueberries, raspberries, and currants
- 10 ounces soft tofu (about 1 container)
- 2 tbsp. honey or agave syrup
- 1 tsp. grated orange zest or lemon zest
- 1/2 tsp. almond extract
- 1 1/2 cups plain, low-fat yogurt
- 2 tsp. vanilla extract
- 1 cup granola of choice

Directions:

Place the berries, tofu, sweetener, citrus zest, and almond extract in a blender or food processor container and blend until smooth. Don't over-process as you want the mixture to be slightly thick.

In a medium bowl, stir together the yogurt and vanilla extract.

To assemble a parfait, place some of the granola on the bottom of a parfait or other glass of choice and top with the yogurt followed by the berry pudding. Repeat so you have two layers of each.

Enjoy!

26. BBQ Chicken Sandwiches with Pickled Vegetables

With the vinegary snap of the vegetable topping and rich fiery kick courtesy of the barbecue sauce, you'd be hard pressed to find a sandwich that's as flavorful and quick as this one.

Makes: 6 servings

Prep: 2 ½ hrs.

Ingredients:

- 1-1/4 cups water, divided
- 1 cup white distilled vinegar
- 1/2 cup white sugar
- 2 1/2 tsp. sea salt, divided
- 1 tsp. mustard seeds (optional)
- 4 cups thinly sliced red cabbage
- 1 small red onion, thinly sliced
- 2 dried ancho chili peppers
- 1/2 cup ketchup
- 2 shallots, chopped
- 2 cloves garlic, minced
- 2 tbsp. cider vinegar
- 1 tbsp. tomato paste
- 1 tbsp. molasses, not blackstrap
- 2 tsp. Worcestershire sauce
- 1/2 tsp. ground cumin
- 1/2 tsp. ground allspice
- 1/4 tsp. freshly ground black pepper
- 4 cups shredded or finely chopped cooked rotisserie chicken
- 6 whole grain buns, split in half

Directions:

To make the pickled vegetables, begin by bringing water to a boil using an electric kettle. In a large heatproof container or bowl, place the vinegar, sugar, 2 tsp. salt, and mustard seeds if using.

Pour in 1 cup boiled water and stir until the sugar has dissolved. Add the cabbage and red onion. Stir to combine, cover, and let stand for at least 2 hours at room temperature, stirring a couple of times.

Meanwhile, start the BBQ sauce by soaking the ancho chili peppers in very hot water for 15 minutes, or until soft. Slice off the stems and remove and reserve the seeds. Place the chili peppers in a blender or food processor container along with as many seeds as you like. If you want a milder sauce, add only a few of the seeds or include more seeds if you want it ¬fiery. Add in the ketchup, 1/4 cup water, shallots, garlic, cider vinegar, tomato paste, molasses, Worcestershire sauce, cumin, allspice, black pepper, and remaining 1/2 tsp. salt, and blend until smooth. Add a little extra water if needed to help with blending.

Place the chicken in a bowl and toss with the barbecue sauce until all the meat is well coated.

Divide the chicken among the bottom halves of the buns, and top with pickled vegetables and remaining bun halves.

Enjoy!

27. Blueberry Dessert Soup

A medley of matched ingredients makes this dessert soup a terrific way to cap off a steamy summer day. It also makes for a good appetizer or snack!

Makes: 6 servings

Prep: 3 hrs. 10 mins

Ingredients:

- 3 cups wild blueberries or 4 cups larger cultivated ones, plus more for garnish
- 3/4 cup plain, 2% Greek yogurt, plus more for garnish
- 1/2 cup unsweetened almond milk
- Juice of 1/2 lemon
- 2 tbsp. chopped fresh mint or 1/2 tsp. peppermint extract
- 2 tbsp. honey or pure maple syrup
- 1 tsp. minced fresh ginger (optional)
- 1/2 tsp. ground allspice

Directions:

Chopped pecans or unsalted raw or roasted almonds, for garnish (optional).

Place the blueberries, yogurt, almond milk, lemon juice, mint, sweetener, ginger if using, and allspice in a blender or food processor container, and process until smooth.

Strain the mixture through a fine-mesh sieve into a bowl to remove any remaining skins.

Refrigerate the soup for at least 3 hours before serving.

To serve, ladle the soup into serving bowls and top with whole blueberries, some Greek yogurt, and chopped nuts if desired.

Enjoy!

28. PB&J Pops

Here's a frosty spin on the iconic sandwich that both adults and young ones will enjoy.

Makes: 4 servings

Prep: 4 hrs. 10 mins

Ingredients:

- 2 cups chopped strawberries
- 2 tbsp. honey or agave syrup
- 2/3 cup evaporated milk
- 1/3 cup plus 1 tbsp. natural unsalted peanut butter
- 1 tsp. vanilla extract

Directions:

Add the strawberries and honey to a food processor or blender container, and blend until smooth. Pour the strawberry puree into a ¬fine-mesh sieve set over a bowl and press down with a spatula.

In a medium bowl, whisk the milk into the peanut butter 2 tbsp. at a time, until silky smooth.

Spoon half of the peanut butter mixture into four standard-size Popsicle molds. Top each with an equal amount of the strawberry puree and ¬finish with the remaining peanut butter. You should have two layers of peanut butter and a single layer of strawberry. Freeze until solid, about 4 hours. If you're having trouble unmolding the Popsicles, run the molds under warm (not hot) water to loosen.

Enjoy!

29. Coffee Ice Cream Float

This dessert is a pretty simple affair, but it's far from an ordinary soda float. This recipe involves steeping the coffee, cocoa, and cardamom together in a coffee press and then stirring in the vanilla once everything has steeped together.

Makes: 2 servings

Prep: 5 mins

Ingredients:

- 2 cups brewed coffee
- 2 tbsp. cocoa powder
- 1/8 tsp. ground cardamom
- 1 tsp. vanilla extract
- 1/2 tsp. ground cinnamon
- 2 generous scoops vanilla, chocolate, or mocha ice cream
- 2 tbsp. chopped almonds or hazelnuts (optional)

Directions:

Place the coffee, cocoa powder, cardamom, and vanilla extract in a blender container and blend until smooth.

Pour into desired glasses or mugs, add ice cream, and top with nuts if using.

Enjoy!

30. Chai Chia Pudding

Thick, naturally sweet and delicious, this chia pudding recipe works well as breakfast, a snack or dessert.

Makes: 6 servings

Prep: 5 ½ hrs.

Ingredients:

- 1 cup raw unsalted cashews
- 4 cups water
- 4 chai tea bags
- 1 cup pitted dates
- 2 tablespoons pure maple syrup (optional)
- 1 ½ teaspoons vanilla extract
- ½ cup chia seeds

Directions:

Place the cashews in a bowl, then cover with the water, and soak for at least 2 hours.

Bring the 4 cups water to a boil in an electric kettle and pour into a large heatproof bowl along with the chai tea bags. Let steep 10 minutes. Remove the tea bags, add the dates to the bowl, and let cool to room temperature.

Drain the cashews and then place them in a blender or food processor container along with the chai and date mixture, maple syrup if using, and vanilla. Blend until very smooth.

Pour in the blended mixture to a large bowl along with the chia seeds and whisk well. Let stand for 15-20 minutes, whisking every few minutes to prevent clumping. Cover the bowl and refrigerate for at least 3 hours before serving.

Enjoy!

Conclusion

There you go! 30 varied, delicious and easy no-cook recipes for when it's too hot to turn on the oven or for when you just can't be bothered to cook. Make sure to try out all the recipes and share them with your friends and family!

About the Author

Allie Allen developed her passion for the culinary arts at the tender age of five when she would help her mother cook for their large family of 8. Even back then, her family knew this would be more than a hobby for the young Allie and when she graduated from high school, she applied to cooking school in London. It had always been a dream of the young chef to study with some of Europe's best and she made it happen by attending the Chef Academy of London.

After graduation, Allie decided to bring her skills back to North America and open up her own restaurant. After 10 successful years as head chef and owner, she decided to sell her business and pursue other career avenues. This monumental decision led Allie to her true calling, teaching. She also started to write e-books for her students to study at home for practice. She is now the proud author of several e-books and gives private and semi-private cooking lessons to a range of students at all levels of experience.

Stay tuned for more from this dynamic chef and teacher when she releases more informative e-books on cooking and baking in the near future. Her work is infused with stores and anecdotes you will love!

Author's Afterthoughts

I can't tell you how grateful I am that you decided to read my book. My most heartfelt thanks that you took time out of your life to choose my work and I hope you find benefit within these pages.

There are so many books available today that offer similar content so that makes it even more humbling that you decided to buying mine.

Tell me what you thought! I am eager to hear your opinion and ideas on what you read as are others who are looking for a good book to buy. Leave a review on Amazon.com so others can benefit from your wisdom!

With much thanks,

Allie Allen

Printed in Great Britain
by Amazon